(above) Saloon car racing is very exciting to watch. The cars must be built to strict rules limiting their power, which means that the racing is very close, as no one car has a strong advantage over the others. The winner is normally the bravest or smartest driver, as long as they can avoid a crash!

(previous page) A Ford Fiesta gets plenty of air during an Italian rally in 2011

Discover.
Learn.
Live.

Lessons for Life

 DRIVING SCHOOL

Mark Philpott

Get in the driving seat!

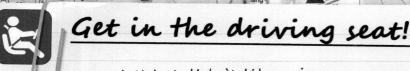

When I was a child, I didn't like going on car journeys. I especially hated going on the Motorway because those journeys seemed like they would never end!

When I turned 17, though, everything changed. I got my own car, and with it the freedom to go virtually anywhere, at any time. Wonderful. Apart from the fact that my old car needed a lot of work to keep it running. I spent a lot of time in overalls getting oily. And then I bought my first Mini, followed by two more! Minis were also unreliable and needed fixing all the time, but I loved driving them so much, it was worth it! It was like being in a go-kart; roundabouts were especially fun.

Cars and driving have played a big part in my life. My granddad was a fuel tanker driver; I have a cousin who is a lorry driver, and one who is a Ford mechanic. My best friend was a London bus driver, and I was a 'white-van man' for a while, delivering across London.

But driving isn't just about fun or work. Cars and trucks have changed people's lives. They have been, and still are, used to spread God's wonderful message of salvation in Jesus. You can find out more about that later.

In this book you will learn about the world of motoring. But you will learn about something much more important, and much more precious – the Gospel of Jesus Christ. You see, by looking at the world of cars and driving, we can learn lessons about Him, about life, and about His Word – the Bible. Read on. What will you learn today?

Mark Philpott, 2022

Granddad in his fuel-soaked overalls, 1950s

First time behind the wheel →

At the National Motor Museum, Beaulieu, 1972

In front of the Queen's car, 1977

Fixing my first car, a 1973 Ford Escort Mk1 1100cc (now a classic, see page 46), 1989

With John Cooper, the creator of the Mini Cooper, 1996

Providing transport at my sister's wedding, 2000

Cadwell Park race circuit in my 1380cc Mini, 2000

Our Citroen diesel 4x4 used for towing our caravan, 2011 (different to driving the Mini!)

Before you start . . . get a Bible
As you read this book, look up the Bible quotes given in the red boxes. God's words are much wiser than mine! If you don't have a 'real' Bible, see if you can download one, or go online.

PSALM 119:105

Thy word is a lamp

105 Thy word is a lam... and a light unto my path
106 I have sworn, ... it, that I will keep t... ments.
107 I am afflicted ... me, O LORD, according...
108 Accept, I bese... will offerings of my ...

Psalm 119

105 Thy word is a lamp unto m... light unto my path.
106 I have sworn, and I will per... that I will keep thy righteo...

A works (factory-prepared) Mini Cooper S rally car with six spot lights, and a sump guard to protect the underside of the engine/gearbox from rocks

CONTENTS
Driving School Curriculum

THE EARLY DAYS
From four legs to four wheels — the first cars

This car from 1896 shows why they were sometimes known as 'horseless carriages'

When horse-power ruled the streets

It is hard now to imagine a time when there were no cars or traffic lights, and streets were cobbled or made of dirt. Horses and walking were the two main ways of getting around, and in cities the amount of horse manure on the streets was sometimes a problem.

Trains had been running since the early 1800s, but the steam engines that powered them were just too impractical for road use. Various inventors had been working hard to develop a new type of engine powered by oil or petrol, rather than steam, and by the late 1800s, the first practical car became a possibility. The first registered design, in 1886, was by a German engineer called Karl Benz, although another German called Gottlieb Daimler built the World's first four-wheeled car around the same time.

Since then, car design has significantly improved. A quick glance at the photo opposite shows that the first cars were uncomfortable and impractical compared to our modern versions, which are reliable and relatively safe. Today, we take things for granted like a roof, heater, electric headlights and an electric starter—early cars had to be started by cranking a handle!

LEARNING POINT

As more effort is put into improving earlier designs, people expect cars to get better and better. We need to beware, though, since there is one thing in life which cannot be improved as time goes on, however much effort is put in; and that is our own human nature, which was ruined by the Fall in the Garden of Eden (Genesis 3). Cars might be improved; but no matter how much we try, we cannot stop being sinners in the sight of a holy God. Many people down through the ages have tried hard to improve themselves and be acceptable to God—look at the Apostle Paul's efforts in Philippians 3:3-7; John Newton, the former slave trader, also tried to reform himself by trying to be good. Eventually, both of them were brought to see that they must stop trying to be righteous, and instead look to Jesus, who <u>did</u> live a perfect life, and who has forgiven the sins of those who trust in Him.

THE BIBLE SAYS . . .
The Apostle Paul said: 'Not having mine own righteousness, which is of the law, but that which is through the faith of Christ.' (Philippians 3:9)

This is a Darracq 8hp vintage car from about 1903. Note the starting (crank) handle just above the number plate

LEARNING TO DRIVE

Every new driver needs instruction of some kind!

DID YOU KNOW?
In the UK, fewer than half of drivers pass the test first time. In 2016, one driver took their 21st test!

Why do cars have three pedals when you only have two feet?

Before you can get behind the wheel, you must pass a theory test. This checks that you know the rules of the road, can spot hazards, and know what to do in common driving situations. When you do eventually get into the driving seat, there is so much to take in. It is like the car makers have made it difficult on purpose! The number of tasks just to get the car moving is hard to remember, especially if you drive a 'manual,' or 'stick' as they call it in the USA. This is because you have to gently adjust both feet on the pedals, as quick movements will 'stall' the car. The three foot pedals in a manual car can be remembered with your ABCs: "A" is for accelerator, which makes the engine 'rev', "B" is for brake, which makes the car stop, and "C" is for clutch, which you must press when you change gear. Two feet are OK for three pedals, because you don't need to 'go' and 'stop' at the same time.

Once moving, you have to be able to steer the car around bends and obstacles, watch out for traffic, cyclists, and pedestrians, whilst reading road signs and listening to your instructor!

DID YOU KNOW?
In some parts of the United States, you only have to be 14 years old to drive legally

LEARNING POINT
The only way to make progress with your driving is to be prepared to take criticism. This is sometimes the hardest part! We must be told where we are going wrong, so we can put it right, remembering that the correction is for our benefit. Are you good at taking criticism? (I'm not, I'm afraid—I still need practice).

The Apostle Peter said to Christians that if they are rightly criticized and take it patiently, what is special about that? But they should seek to take it patiently if they are criticized even if they **haven't** done anything wrong. How difficult is that for us! We always want to justify ourselves don't we? But this isn't God's way. Jesus showed amazing humility, because He put up with sinners constantly criticising Him for doing wrong, when He wasn't (Hebrews 12:3). He was perfect. We are not perfect, we fail, and we sin every day. But God has forgiven the sins of those who trust the perfect One, who never answered back.

THE BIBLE SAYS . . .
My son, despise not the chastening [loving correction] of the LORD; neither be weary of his correction.' (Proverbs 3:11)

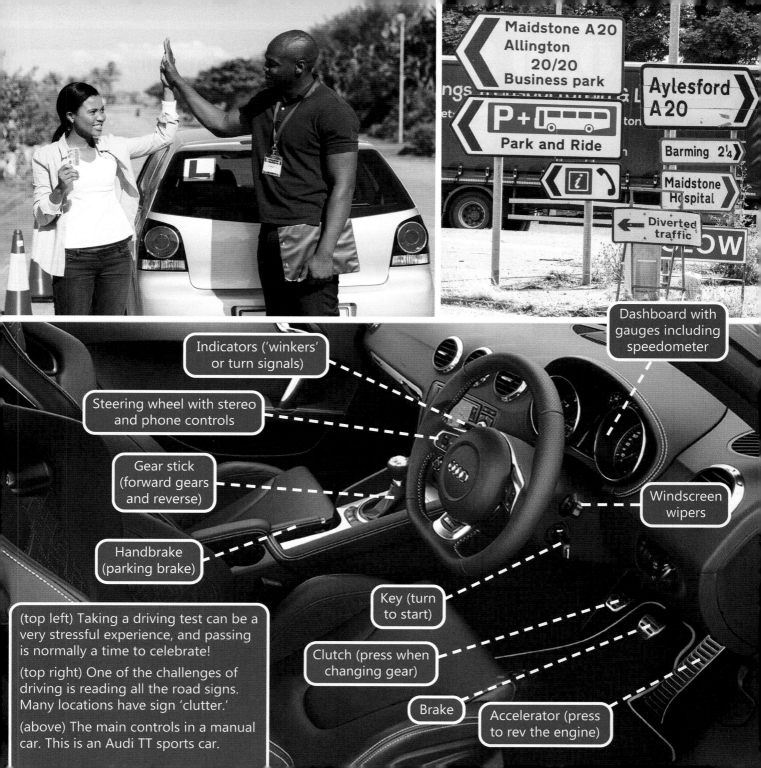

Indicators ('winkers' or turn signals)

Steering wheel with stereo and phone controls

Gear stick (forward gears and reverse)

Handbrake (parking brake)

Dashboard with gauges including speedometer

Windscreen wipers

Key (turn to start)

Clutch (press when changing gear)

Brake

Accelerator (press to rev the engine)

(top left) Taking a driving test can be a very stressful experience, and passing is normally a time to celebrate!

(top right) One of the challenges of driving is reading all the road signs. Many locations have sign 'clutter.'

(above) The main controls in a manual car. This is an Audi TT sports car.

Maidstone A20
Allington
20/20
Business park

Aylesford A20

P + 🚌
Park and Ride

Barming 2¼

Maidstone Hospital

Diverted traffic

SLOW

ROAD SIGNS
Helping drivers to find their way and keep safe

Do you know what these signs mean?

For each sign below, work out its meaning by looking up the three Bible quotes. One of the three quotes has a clue in it; can you find the right one? The answers are shown on **page 77** near the end of the book.

(KJV / NKJV / NIV / ESV. Some other Bible versions may differ.)

The answers are shown on **page 77** near the end of the book.

DID YOU KNOW?

The shape of a road sign often tells you its purpose. The most common ones are:

Hazard: warning of danger ahead

Order: something you must do or not do

Helpful information such as directions

1

Genesis 17:4
Exodus 40:35
Leviticus 1:7

2

Deuteronomy 28:7
Acts 2:3
Hebrews 8:12

3

Galatians 5:1
Ecclesiastes 2:4
Luke 8:33

4

Deuteronomy 17:16
Genesis 1:3
Psalm 23:6

5

Joel 2:15
Amos 9:10
Obadiah 17

6

Judges 5:3
Revelation 6:16
Colossians 3:23

7

Matthew 28:18
Mark 8:37
Luke 11:46

8

Joshua 6:3
Esther 4:14
Proverbs 26:1

9

1 John 1:4
Deuteronomy 5:32
Psalm 2:6

10

Matthew 7:14
Isaiah 40:31
Acts 28:28

In the UK, it is a common sight to see road signs warning of animals on the road - typically sheep, cows, horses and deer. Around the World, the range of animals is often more exotic!

CAUTION
Antelope entering highway at 55 mph.

Voer van Bobbejane Verbode
Feeding of Baboons Prohibited

Beware! Qaphela!
For your own safety, this Hide:

PLEASE BRAKE FOR SNAKES

NEXT 8 km

CAUTION NEXT 5 km

LEARNING POINT When driving, how important it is to keep an eye out for road signs! Failing to pay attention to what the signs say could cause an accident, or even death. These signs are provided by the Highway Authority, because they know what is ahead, and they put the signs there as either a help, an order, or a warning.

The Old Testament is a collection of writings which all point forwards to the time when Jesus, the Son of God, would come into the World. Jesus says of the Old Testament writers that many of them were prophets; that is, they spoke for God to the people about what was to come. The writings were like signs, pointing the people to the coming Chosen One, Jesus. Some of the people in Israel had read the 'signs', and they immediately recognised Jesus as the Son of God when He came into the World—see the story of Simeon and Anna in Luke 2:25-38.

There were, however, wicked people, who did not believe the 'signs' given in the Old Testament about Jesus. They wanted extra signs to confirm who He was. Many people are like that today. They do not believe the Bible, and they do not want to. But this will end badly, as Jesus explained in the parable of the rich man and the beggar in Luke 16:19-31. Do you believe what God has said about Jesus?

THE BIBLE SAYS...
'If they hear not Moses and the prophets, neither will they be persuaded, though one rose from the dead.' (Luke 16:31)

In Matthew 2, the wise men came to find Jesus because they had seen His star, and realised it was the sign given in Numbers 24:17.

NIGHT DRIVING
Staying on the road in the dark

Streetlights, headlights, or cat's eyes . . . as long as you can see the road ahead

When I was young and used to drive around with my friends in the car, sometimes we would get up to some foolish pranks. It was not uncommon to be driving along on a country lane at night, and the front seat passenger would quickly lean over and turn off the headlights, plunging the road ahead into complete darkness. The light was quickly turned back on, but it was enough to give a complete fright, and make you realise how helpless you were without light shining to make the way ahead clear.

Cars have been fitted with headlamps from the earliest days, as without them they cannot be driven anywhere at night where there is no street lighting.

LEARNING POINT
All down the ages, man has realised the need of having light to be able to see in the dark. The Bible talks a great deal about lamps and light. The Psalmist said that God's Word (the Bible) is like a lamp which shines on the path where he is walking (Psalm 119:105). Jesus is called the Word (John 1) and He said, "I am come a light into the world" (John 12:46) so that whoever believes on Him would not be in darkness.

What is this darkness? It is not realizing the truth about ourselves, that we are lost sinners, and that God is holy and righteous and He must punish sin. What is this Light? It is Jesus Himself, who shines into the hearts of lost sinners, so they can see the truth about themselves and about God. And most of all, this Light is seeing Jesus as the One who came to seek and to save those who were lost; those who were sitting in darkness to bring them into His marvellous light, to go on their way rejoicing.

DID YOU KNOW?
The first 'cat's eyes'—the road studs found in the middle of country roads and on high speed roads—were invented in 1934 by Percy Shaw from Halifax, UK. He took his inspiration from the way that cat's eyes reflect light at night. The studs allow the driver to more easily see the road ahead in the dark, making driving safer.

THE BIBLE SAYS . . .
'I will make darkness light before them.' (Isaiah 42:16)

Jesus came 'to give light to them that sit in darkness... to guide our feet into the way of peace.' (Luke 1:79)

Rally cars are fitted with bright spotlights which light up the road hundreds of metres/yards ahead

Driving in the dark and wet is very tiring. Having road lighting, as well as headlamps, really helps

THE KNOWLEDGE
London taxi drivers ("cabbies")—human satnav

The World's toughest cabbie test

Nowadays we get used to using satnav to help us take the quickest route to our destination. Satnav isn't always reliable in cities because tall buildings block the signal, and they don't always deal well with road closures and differing delays at junctions (there can be a big queue turning right, but not left, and satnav cannot tell). Taxis can also use bus lanes to bypass queues, and satnav cannot take that into account either. Plus there is the benefit that cabbies know all the landmarks, hotels, and attractions which make their knowledge so useful for visitors.

Satnav is used by many drivers around the World

There are thousands of streets and landmarks within a six mile radius of Charing Cross. Anyone who wants to drive an iconic London cab must memorize them all. This is known as 'the Knowledge'. This became a requirement for taxi drivers in 1865, and it typically takes 3-4 years. Medical scans have shown that cabbies' brains get larger after they have learnt the Knowledge!

LEARNING POINT

What sort of knowledge do you fill your head with? It is great to have a thirst for knowledge. But we can also spend a lot of time learning useless information.

There is an amazing book which is always worth our time to study. A book which recounts amazing stories of fire coming down from the sky; of giants being beheaded; of a talking donkey; of plagues of locusts; of the sun going backwards in the sky; and people being brought back from the dead. Yes, the Bible. It is much more than a story book though. It is the history of the World; it explains why there is so much trouble; and what is the meaning of life—that we were created by God to serve Him. Most importantly of all, it reveals a God determined to have a people with Him in Heaven, even though He had to come to the Earth and die a painful death for them. This is the knowledge which changes lives for time and eternity.

THE BIBLE SAYS . . .
2 Timothy 3:15 says the Bible is able to make 'wise unto salvation through faith which is in Christ Jesus.'

May we not be like those who are 'ever learning, and never able to come to a knowledge of the truth.' (2 Timothy 3:7)

London taxis are known as 'black cabs,' but some aren't black

A London taxi enters Parliament Square in front of Elizabeth Tower, better known as 'Big Ben'

DID YOU KNOW?
A brand new London 'black cab' costs over £55,000. All new cabs must now be electric.

BLUES AND TWOS
Getting to an emergency as fast as possible

DID YOU KNOW?
The phrase 'blues and twos' comes from the old blue rotating lamps and two-tone horns, in use before the modern sirens and light bars

"Hang on, we'll be there!"

Whether it is a medical crisis, a spreading fire, or a robbery in progress, there is a need to get officers to where they are needed without delay.

When travelling at high speed, especially through towns and cities, there is risk of having a crash on the way to the scene (see photo right), so emergency services do what they can to avoid this happening. From the earliest days of the fire brigade, bells were used to warn road users to get out of the way. Nowadays the emergency services fit their vehicles with light bars, housing super-bright flashing blue (and/or red) lights, and use loud sirens with varying sound patterns to grab attention. Crucially, drivers have to undergo intensive training in how to drive safely at speed in all kinds of situations. If help is sent, it must arrive safely—and when it does, what a difference it can make to those in difficulty.

LEARNING POINT

If your family or friends are in trouble, do you want to help them, and as quickly as possible? We sometimes fail our friends, but God doesn't fail. He helps without any *unnecessary* delay, when sincere prayer is offered to Him in time of need (Luke 18:1-8).

In John 11:1-46 there is a strange and remarkable account of one of Jesus' friends, called Lazarus, falling very ill. His friends sent for Jesus to come quickly and heal him. But Jesus did not go straight away. How strange this seemed. Eventually Lazarus died and was buried, so the situation seemed hopeless when Jesus arrived. But this delay was to be for God's glory, as it allowed Jesus to do an amazing miracle, and raise Lazarus from the dead. God's help is always at the right time.

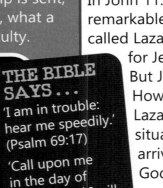

THE BIBLE SAYS...

'I am in trouble: hear me speedily.' (Psalm 69:17)

'Call upon me in the day of trouble, and I will deliver [save you].' (Psalm 50:15)

Some police forces have a supercar on hand for high-speed chases

POLICE 777 الشرطة

A car fire is put out on the M5 motorway

A common scene; a NYFD (New York Fire Department) fire truck on one of New York's wide one-way streets

SPEEDING
Breaking the law by driving too fast

Have you got an excuse?

One of the first lessons which new motorists learn is to avoid getting speeding tickets! Preferably this should be done by carefully looking out for road signs, and driving well within the speed limit. However, some motorists take a different approach, and accept an occasional fine as a hazard. In days gone by, speeding motorists would be stopped by the police and, provided they were good natured with the officer, the policeman would often allow them on their way with just a proverbial slap on the wrist—after being firmly put in their place, of course! Nowadays though, things are different. Speed cameras have replaced police officers, and there is no officer to plead with. If you see a flash in your rear view mirror, you wait 7-10 days for the buff envelope in the mail.

Australian V8 Holden *Highway Patrol* car with advice for drivers

HIGHWAY PATROL HWP151

There is no excuse

LEARNING POINT

STATE POLICE

OREGON STATE

E267286

Drivers might not see speed limit signs, and there might be good excuses given for speeding. But God says that when every single person stands before His throne on the Day of Judgement, there will be no excuse for saying, 'I didn't realise God exists; I could not see Him; I did not know what He expected of me.' No. The Bible tells us that there will be no excuse because it is obvious that there is a Creator who has made everything and owns us. If we look up at the stars, or at a flower, we should realise. But our evil hearts reject God. Even if we believe in God, no-one can say they are perfect; we have all broken God's holy law. But there is good news. The Bible also says that all who are brought to trust in Jesus will be found 'not guilty.' Jesus Christ has put Himself in the place of needy sinners.

(main image) Gatso speed camera in widespread use in the UK.

(below) Drivers have so much to look out for that speed limit signs can easily be missed. Where there have been a high number of accidents, some signs are given a yellow backing board to make them stand out.

THE BIBLE SAYS...

'The invisible things of him from the creation of the World are clearly seen, being understood by the things that are made, even his eternal power and Godhead; so that they are without excuse.' (Romans 1:20)

'All have sinned, and come short of the glory of God.' (Romans 3:23)

DID YOU KNOW?

The first ever speeding ticket was given in 1896 in Paddock Wood, Kent, UK, when a policeman chased a car 5 miles on his bicycle. The speed? 8mph — 6mph over the 2mph speed limit!

FREEWAYS
Wide roads for high traffic volumes

DID YOU KNOW?
One of the widest roads in the World is the Katy Freeway, part of the Interstate 10 route in Texas, USA. In places it is 26 lanes wide and carries over 1 million vehicles a week.

Go with the flow

Whether called freeways, motorways, or expressways, these modern roads are designed to carry large volumes of traffic for long distances and at relatively high speed compared with old roads, streets, and country lanes. The roads are built so that they do not have junctions like roundabouts or traffic lights; instead roads pass over or under using bridges so as not to stop the flow of traffic. Once you are on the motorway, you have to keep going in the same direction, and can only leave at the signed exits (off-ramps). Also, because tractors, parking, pedestrians and cycles are not allowed, there is nothing to delay the traffic. In reality, however, the roads are so attractive that they end up carrying more traffic than they were designed for, leading to lots of congestion.

Arizona, USA: three freeways merge just down from this stretch of road which is 11 lanes wide

(right) The M25 around London, the busiest road in the UK and voted its worst because of the congestion

There are plenty of religious people who think that they are on their way to Heaven. But are they? Are you, or I? What an important question!

Jesus said that there is a broad way (wide road) which leads to destruction, and there are many which go that way (Matthew 7:13-14). What is this broad way? It is when men and women think they can follow the crowd and do what religious leaders tell them to do, without checking if it is what God has said. Normally it involves doing something to try and earn a place in Heaven by working hard. Or there are others who think that, if they just do their best to be good, God will be pleased with them (Luke 18:11-12). They forget that God must punish every sin—saying "sorry" isn't enough for a holy God. This is the broad way—going the way that seems good to you.

What does the Bible say is **the way** to get to Heaven? It is called a narrow way, because the only way to be saved is to trust Jesus ALONE, believing in Him. Like a narrow country lane, not many people go that way, but it leads to eternal life.

THE BIBLE SAYS...
Jesus said, 'I am the way, the truth, and the life.' (John 14:6)

'Ask for the old paths, where is the good way, and ... find rest for your souls.' (Jeremiah 6:16)

DID YOU KNOW?
The first motorway in the UK opened in 1958. It was called the Preston Bypass and is now part of the M6.

A single-track country lane in Hertfordshire, UK; slow in contrast to the other roads on this page—but very pleasant!

The Golden Gate Bridge in San Francisco, California, USA, carries six lanes of traffic as part of both Route 101 and California State Route 1. It was opened in 1937.

EXTREME ROADS
Where the going gets tough

Roads for every situation

Although many complain of potholes, for the most part roads in the developed West (UK, USA, Australia, etc.) are relatively kind to cars and their drivers. They are 'metalled' (surfaced) and generally wide enough for two cars to pass each other. However, in places such as Africa most of the roads away from cities are dirt roads which can become extremely muddy and difficult to drive along after rain, with a constant hazard of getting stuck.

Mountains, hills and valleys also create some interesting situations for getting vehicles across them. Building a road straight up a steep slope isn't normally sensible, because this would often lead to brakes overheating on the way down, which is obviously extremely dangerous. It is also difficult for vehicles to go up steep slopes without burning out the clutch and overheating the engine. For this reason it is normal to build 'switchbacks' or hairpin bends, which gradually climb on a more gentle gradient. These are not easy to drive though, as the bends are very sharp and often steeper on the inside of the turn.

LEARNING POINT

Life is like a journey. How easy our journey is depends on the quality of the road. This World has been ruined by sin, and everything can seem an uphill struggle. We get bogged down in everyday life and feel like we aren't getting anywhere. The hardest hill to climb, though, is getting to Heaven. Plenty of people try to get there by doing good to others, or doing what they think will please God. But the way is impossible. However, there is help. Where does the help come from? The Bible says that Jesus came to Earth to make a way to get to Heaven. Every obstacle would be overcome. He would straighten out every twisty way, make smooth every rough way, and remove every steep hill, so that nothing would stop the salvation of His people—Jesus is the Way. Sin is what prevents anyone getting to Heaven, but Jesus has paid the price for every sin of each one He has saved.

THE BIBLE SAYS...
'Every mountain and hill shall be brought low; and the crooked shall be made straight, and the rough ways shall be made smooth; and all flesh shall see the salvation of God.' (Luke 3:5-6)

(above left) A typical African dirt road

(above) A super-straight road in Monument Valley, Utah, USA. This road is so easy to drive on compared with the other two on this page.

(below) Some of the 11 hairpin bends on the Trollstigen Pass, Norway

A NEW CAR
The 2nd most expensive purchase most people ever make

Clean, shiny and reliable; but for how long?

There is something special about getting a brand new car; a perfectly clear windscreen to look out of, clean carpets, shiny paint, no empty sweet packets in the door pockets, and—best of all—that 'new car' smell! It is also good to know that (hopefully) the car will be reliable, and run for many miles trouble-free.

Nothing lasts for ever though. Even new cars go wrong. That is why good car dealers offer a **warranty**, so that if anything goes wrong they will pay for it to be fixed, which gives the buyer peace of mind. These *new car* warranties normally last between 3 and 7 years.

LEARNING POINT

A warranty is a written pledge by the seller to repair or replace something which was bought, for a period of time from its sale. But what happens when the warranty period expires? The owner is now left by themselves to sort out the problem, and to pay for it. An endless warranty would be much too expensive. Car dealers just cannot afford to make promises which never run out.

What a mercy that God's promises are not like new car warranties! His promises never expire. It doesn't matter how much time passes, because God does not change, and that means that His promises to His people, and those to everyone who lives in the World, will never break.

WHERE ARE THESE PROMISES IN THE BIBLE?

Match each promise 1-3 with one of the 3 chapters A-C. **Answers: p77**

1 'Although my house be not so with God, yet he *has* made with me an everlasting covenant, ordered in all things, and sure: for this is all my salvation.'

2 'This shall be the covenant that I will make with the house of Israel... I will put my law ... in their hearts; and will be their God, and they shall be my people.'

3 'The bow shall be in the cloud; and I will look upon it, that I may remember the everlasting covenant between God and every living creature.'

A GENESIS 9   **B** 2 SAMUEL 23   **C** JEREMIAH 31

DID YOU KNOW?
A covenant is a solemn promise

Car makers take publicity photographs to make their products look appealing

Car showrooms are clean and bright to make the cars look as attractive as possible

BUYER BEWARE

Buying a used car: will it be a good one?

A Damask Red Mini 1275GT just like the one in this story

What you (think you) see isn't always what you get

Buying a used car is one of those things in life which always evokes mixed feelings; sure, it is exciting to get something 'new' (to you), but will it live up to expectations? My friend Andy and I went to look at a classic Mini 1275GT for him to consider buying. He saw it and wanted it! It was an attractive deep red and it made a tremendous 'brrr' sound through its sports exhaust. But little known to us (we should have looked a little harder), everything wasn't as it seemed. One winter's day, Andy was driving at speed around a roundabout, and after heavy rain and fallen leaves the drains had blocked, and he had no choice but to drive through a very large and deep puddle. All of a sudden, he was soaked as a wave of filthy freezing cold water showered him from head to toe! He had the shock of his life! Underneath the thick layers of carpet, the floor had already rusted away, leaving a large hole.

Wise buyers carefully check a car over, and buy a car they think will give years of good service.

DID YOU KNOW?
In the UK, cars which are more than 3 years old must take an annual test to check they are safe to drive. This is known as an MOT test, after the Ministry of Transport as it was then called when the test was introduced in 1960.

LEARNING POINT
We have to be so careful that we don't make decisions with our *hearts* (what we desire) instead of our *heads* (that which we know to be right). It is all too easy to buy a car because of an attractive colour, or nice shiny wheels, or lots of comforts. This applies in all areas of life. Do not listen to the World's advice to 'follow your heart'! Satan tempts us to desire things, and we convince ourselves that these things will make us happy. But so often we find the enjoyment of those things hollow. Perhaps they don't live up to our expectations, and in the end we are left poorer and less happy. There is a treasure, though, which doesn't rust, or disappoint, and that is Jesus Himself. If we know Him, love Him and trust Him, we have all we can desire, and He will never disappoint us! He will never let us down.

THE BIBLE SAYS ...
In Matthew 6:19-20, Jesus tells His followers not to gather treasures on the Earth, where rust corrupts. Instead, 'lay up for yourselves treasure in heaven.'

TRUCKS
Reliable workhorses for every job

Delivering and shifting everything, day in, day out

Clothes, food, books, phones ... nearly everything you have bought or been given has probably travelled some of its journey on a truck. Trucks are vehicles designed to carry large quantities of goods at a time, and so are often referred to as Heavy Goods Vehicles (HGVs). Although fully laden trucks are slow up hill, they have very large and powerful diesel engines which can haul loads weighing 24 tonnes or more, that is 10,500 bricks, which is enough to build a house!

Trucks are built for a wide variety of roles. Manufacturers build the basic frame (chassis) with driver's cab and engine; and then specialist companies build the bodies and trailers which are needed for their intended use. The page opposite shows the four main truck layouts, and if you turn over you will see examples of some of the most common truck types.

Lorries are often fitted with tail-lifts, ramps, cranes, or even forklift trucks to help offload goods.

LEARNING POINT

What are you good at? Everyone is different. Some people are good at sports. Some are good at science. Others are good at cooking, or fixing things, or even talking! God has made us all unique, and given us each things we can do.

Churches are made up of lots of different people, and each can help in various ways. Some are preachers; some visit the sick; some look after the building; some teach children. Everyone is important; everyone has something to offer. And, most importantly, everyone can pray!

In the Bible it says that God has carefully crafted every believer to be just how He wants them to be. He has made them to do the work He wants them to do, just like the trucks are made with a specific purpose in mind. So, if you love the Lord, you follow Him, you are baptised, you join a church, and you serve God as well as you can. This is God's will for His people.

THE BIBLE SAYS ...
'For we are his workmanship, created in Christ Jesus unto good works.' (Ephesians 2:10)

RIGID

Driver's cab and load section in one body. This one has a crane to load and offload goods.

ARTICULATED

'Artic' for short. These comprise of a 'tractor' unit including the driver's cab and diesel engine (the red section), plus a trailer which can be unhooked and swapped (the light blue section).

DRAWBAR

A rigid lorry plus a steerable trailer

A lorry with more than one trailer

ROADTRAIN

TRUCK TYPES

On this page:
Refuse collection
Parcels (or removals)
Bulk foods
Car transporter
Fuel tanker
Tipper
Livestock (sheep)
Mobile crane
Chilled / refrigerated
Breakdown recovery
Snowplough / gritter
Motorhome (RV)

apollorv.co

On this page:

Horse transport
Fire engine
Flatbed
Curtainsider
Roadsweeper
Container lorry
Low loader
Cement mixer
Skip lorry
Traffic management

How many of these types can you spot on your next long journey?

OVERLOADED?

How much weight can a vehicle handle?

DID YOU KNOW?
Have you heard the expression "a shed load"? This comes from a lorry shedding (losing) its load onto the road.

"If it fits, load it on!"

Perhaps you have seen someone on their way home from a DIY shop, with planks of wood poking out of the car window. Or maybe someone has bought a second-hand sofa and lashed it to the roof of their car. If this has been done unsafely, they might be stopped by the police.

Overloading trucks is dangerous as it can lead to tonnes of goods being shed onto the road and can cause a major pile-up and long delays. Overweight lorries also damage bridges and the road surface. In the UK there are weighbridges, which are giant weighing scales, which can check if a vehicle is overweight. These are often found at docks or large factories.

LEARNING POINT

A Volvo lorry about to leave the docks is checked on a weighbridge to ensure the load is within legal limits

One of the dangers of religion is that preachers, priests, rabbis or other leaders might teach that the way to get to Heaven, or to lead a good religious life, is to keep lots of laws, and do this, that, or the other. This way, they say, we will be accepted by God. Sometimes they guilt people into working really hard, saying that you *would* work harder if you loved God. If we listen to them, and try and do everything they say, we will end up feeling guilty, because we fail to be good enough. But it won't help us get to Heaven! What does Jesus say in Luke 11:46 about the religious leaders of His day? (Read from v39.)

Jesus loves His people and does not make them feel guilty about their efforts! He lived a perfect life, which no-one else can do, and died to save them. He has done all the work they need to get to Heaven. God's people are not His slaves! They love Him for what He has done and work joyfully for their Master in Heaven (Romans 12:1).

THE BIBLE SAYS...
Jesus said, 'My yoke is easy, and my burden is light.' (Matthew 11:30) {yoke: wooden harness put on an animal for pulling a load, e.g. plough}

It is not uncommon to see vehicles overloaded in many parts of the World, especially in poorer countries. There is a completely different approach to safety!

ABNORMAL LOADS
Delivering huge items safely

How do you deliver something as large as a wind turbine?

Trucks are great at moving large quantities of goods, but some things are just too long, too wide, too tall or too heavy for a regular truck. Every year there are items such as wind turbines, electricity sub-stations, parts of oil rigs (see photos), steel chimneys and a myriad other things which need delivering. Some companies have heavy-duty lorries and they work with the Highway Authority, and sometimes the police, to carefully plan an appropriate route well ahead of time. This is because very heavy loads cannot go over weak bridges; very tall loads cannot pass under low bridges; and very wide or long loads cannot make some turns without taking down signs or traffic lights. On the day, the abnormal load must be led by an 'escort'—this is a vehicle which goes ahead and checks that the way is clear. The truck driver follows, carefully and slowly. Without the escort, the load cannot move.

A police vehicle leads the convoy to clear the way

LEARNING POINT

Christians are followers of Jesus Christ. The Bible likens them to sheep who follow their shepherd, because they trust Him. Read Psalm 23; David talks about the LORD leading him, in both pleasant and dangerous places; but David trusted God to keep him safe.

Jesus is called the Good Shepherd who cares for His sheep. Some sheep are old, or soon to give birth to lambs ('with young'), and cannot move quickly. This is a way of saying that some Christians are weak, or afraid, or not able to deal with difficult things. But Jesus knows, and is so caring that He makes sure that He gently leads them on in their lives day-by-day. He ensures that none is pushed too far, and that everyone has enough strength for each day (Deuteronomy 33:25). Like the escort vehicle, Jesus goes only where His people can manage, at a pace they can deal with. He has also been ahead and prepared a way for them, in life and in death (Hebrews 6:20).

THE BIBLE SAYS...
'He shall feed his flock like a shepherd ... and shall gently lead those that are with young.' (Isaiah 40:11)

See Exodus 23:20 where God sent an Angel (Christ) before the Israelites.

An extra-long load is carefully taken through the streets of Wick, Scotland, on its way to be used in the North Sea oil industry. Note that the many small wheels on the trailer steer to get it round the bend.

MISSION SUPPORT

Helping take the Gospel to those in need

Travel in rural Africa is rough

In 2012, James Gudgeon, a minister from Hastings in the UK, felt led by the Lord to go to Mombasa in Kenya to preach the good news of Jesus Christ and help the local poor. He sold his home, packed his Land Rover into a shipping container, and then flew out there with his wife and children. The Land Rover proved to be of great use, not only helping James get to churches and rural villages to preach, but to help transport building materials. Travel is difficult because roads are very rough and delivery services and public transport are poor.

James' vision for the mission work grew, requiring construction of several new buildings and underground water storage, so an old Bedford army truck was bought to transport the tonnes of materials which would be needed. Like the Land Rover, it is a 4x4 which allows it to keep going even in the wet and muddy conditions of the rainy season.

The Land Rover is ideal for mission work because it is rugged and can carry heavy loads

LEARNING POINT

Mission work is tough. All those involved must commit themselves to the Lord in prayer every day asking for help, strength and safe keeping. James and his wife have worked tirelessly, because they want to tell people the truth about Jesus, and show love to the people in Kenya. The vehicles enable them to reach and help more people. How thankful they must be for having them! The truck was purchased using donations from loving Christians. What a difference it makes when the Lord puts it in people's hearts to give generously to His work!

The truck has helped them to build this large water storage tank

Mombasa Mission

THE BIBLE SAYS...

The Apostle Paul said, 'Having therefore obtained help of God, I continue unto this day, witnessing to both small [lowly] and great [important].' (Acts 26:22)

(top left) The truck has shifted tonnes of stone for building a new road to the mission station, to keep access in the wet season. Dirt tracks and roads become waterlogged (left).

(top centre/right) James with local children; and in the truck

(below left) The truck makes a good preaching platform

(bottom left) The 'Landy' pulls another vehicle out of the mud

(bottom centre) Giving 'locals' a lift in the Land Rover

(below right) The mission station, built and maintained using the Land Rover and the Bedford army truck

One man's journey to strengthen Christians being persecuted

In 1955, a young Dutchman went to a communist youth rally in Poland, which at that time was one of the countries under the control of the Soviet Union. (These countries were said to be behind the Iron Curtain, because you couldn't easily get in or out.) But this man wasn't a communist: he was a Christian. He came to be known as Brother Andrew, and the trip was to change his life.

It was against the law to take Bibles into countries behind the Iron Curtain. He found churches desperately in need of Bibles. Above all, he found Christians who felt alone and who thought the rest of the World had forgotten them. He went to a Baptist church in Warsaw and after the meeting the pastor said, "We want to thank you for being here. We feel as if we are all alone in our struggle [to keep worshipping Jesus against the will of the government]."

At the end of the trip, Brother Andrew prayed about what God wanted him to do. He opened his Bible at Revelation 3:2, the verse which he came to see as his mission: "Wake Up! Strengthen what remains and is about to die." He saw that the churches had hardly any life in them; some were ready to give up their religion, and they needed encouragement.

How could he get so many Bibles to these struggling Christians? He was poor and could not afford a car. But God provided one, by putting it in the heart of friends to donate their nearly-new VW Beetle. For years after, he was to drive many times behind the Iron Curtain, putting his life on the line to smuggle Bibles.

The most dangerous part of his mission work was the border crossings. He hid the Bibles in the car, and as he approached the armed guards, who would search the car, he prayed:

> "Lord, in my luggage I have Scripture I want to take to Your children. When You were on Earth, You made blind eyes see. Now, I pray, make seeing eyes blind. Do not let the guards see those things You do not want them to see."

God answered his prayer. Every time.

His blue VW Beetle became known as 'the miracle car', for its ability to miraculously keep going. When the engine did eventually die, after nearly 200,000km, he did not have enough money to fix it, yet out of nowhere the exact amount of money was given a few seconds just before the repair bill was due. This was another sign that the work was God's.

"Don't choose what pleases you. Please the One who chooses you."
Brother Andrew

Open Doors

Brother Andrew, real name Andrew van der Bijl, and his amazing story 'God's Smuggler' (over 10 million copies sold)

OVER TEN MILLION COPIES SOLD

GOD'S SMUGGLER
'S MISSION - TO CHANGE THE WORLD
Brother Andrew

24·46·VT

LEARNING POINT

As the work grew, Brother Andrew was joined by others to smuggle thousands of Bibles to Christians in Communist countries. His small Dutch mission has become an international charity called 'Open Doors,' working in more than 60 nations to strengthen the persecuted Church. His work, of spreading God's Word to those who were thirsty for it (ready to receive it), truly was a blessing to them. Do you or I feel our thirst for the good news of God's Word?

THE BIBLE SAYS . . .
'As cold waters to a thirsty soul, so is good news from a far country.' (Proverbs 25:25)

CLASSIC CARS
Old cars lovingly kept in 'like new' condition

(right) Two gleaming Ford Escort Mk1s from the 1970s at a classic car show

(below right) Particular attention is often given to having lots of chrome-plated parts on the engine—especially on American cars like this one

'Old' doesn't mean worse than 'new'

In recent years, it has become very popular to own a classic car—a car of any age which isn't made any more, although cars from the 1950s to the 1980s are most popular. There are many reasons why people like owning classic cars. Some like to restore them; some like to maintain them because, unlike modern cars, they don't have computers or electronics; some like their style; for some people it just reminds them of the 'good old days' before modern life became madly busy. There are a huge variety of classic cars, from old Ferraris to ordinary family cars. Some even have former police patrol cars, retired race cars, or buses!

One thing owners usually have in common is a desire to keep their 'pride and joy' very clean, especially if going to a classic car show. These shows are popular with enthusiasts and the general public alike. A close look, even under the bonnet, won't reveal any dirt!

This Austin Healey looks almost as good as it did when it rolled off the production line

DID YOU KNOW?
In 2018, a 1963 Ferrari 250 GTO sold for $70m!

LEARNING POINT

If you compare a classic car with your family's car, you are likely to realise how clean the classic car is! Even if you get down on your knees and closely inspect the wheels and underneath of the classic car, it will still look clean. There are classic car competitions, where judges look even inside the wheel valve dust caps to see if they are clean. But even a judge cannot look deep inside the exhaust pipe or engine; there will be some dirt, no matter how hidden from view. The classic cars are like us. We might be proud, and think we are clean (free from sin) because we try and be well behaved. But God sees everything. He can see inside us. Even <u>one</u> sin makes us too unclean for Heaven. We cannot make ourselves clean, but Jesus can completely wash away the stain of sin.

THE BIBLE SAYS...
'Wash me, and I shall be whiter than snow.' (Psalm 51:7)

THE MIGHTY MINI
The small car with a big heart

★★★★

DID YOU KNOW?
From its launch in 1959 to the end of production in 2000, 5.3 million Minis were sold. It has been voted the 2nd greatest car of all time behind the iconic Ford Model T.

E MORRIS MINI-MINOR AND AUSTIN SEVEN

Mini in name, but not in nature

The humble Mini was expected to be just a practical car for families. Its design was unique when it appeared on the market in 1959, as it was the first small car to have the inside space of a larger car. The designer, Sir Alec Issigonis, had no idea how popular his car would be. Not only was it cheap to run, but it was great fun behind the wheel, easy to drive and park on narrow city streets, and it had a cheeky character all of its own. Before long, many famous people had bought one and it became *the* car to own.

A man called John Cooper saw the car's potential for competition and he persuaded the Mini manufacturer BMC to modify them. The Mini Cooper was born, and soon became a motorsport legend. With the right expertise, the Mini could be turned into a giant-killer; they beat Porsches and other sports cars to win the Monte Carlo Rally four* years in a row, and they were a common sight jostling with huge American V8-powered cars around race tracks.

LEARNING POINT

The term 'giant-killer' comes from the story of David and Goliath. David was the youngest of 8 brothers, and he was only a youth when he killed the giant. Similarly, Gideon was the youngest in his family, and he felt feeble and unimportant, but God chose him to lead Israel to defeat their enemies. God often uses the humble, the weak and the lowly to do His work. Look especially at the coming of Jesus into the World. He was born to poor parents, and worked as a carpenter. He could have come as a beautiful, strong superhero, but He came as a 'nobody' in the eyes of the worldly. Yet there has never been anyone like Him. No-one has been so humble and yet so mighty. Jesus has won the victory over the giants of sin, Satan and death!

THE BIBLE SAYS...
In Philippians 2:5-11, it says that Jesus came into the World like a servant, but every knee will one day bow to Him.

In Hebrews 11, see how God's people 'out of weakness were made strong.'

A rally Mini in action

(main image) The three official winners of the Monte Carlo Rally, Mini Coopers 33 EJB (1964), AJB 44B (1965) and LBL 6D (1967)

*In 1966, Minis came 1st, 2nd and 3rd, but they do not feature in official records because the French organisers promptly disqualified all 3 on a minor technical detail, so a French Citroen 'won' instead.

(below) Minis have become a popular enthusiast's car, and there are many owners clubs and organised outings to enjoy everything 'Mini'

(main image) Mini racing is always entertaining. Here are race-prepared 1275cc Minis fighting for position.

(above) A Mk1 Mini Cooper nips at the heels of a much larger and more powerful Ford Cortina. This was a common sight in 1960s track racing.

RALLYING

Dodging trees and deadly drops at 100mph

When things go sideways...

Rallies consist of a series of timed stages, over all sorts of surfaces such as gravel, mud, dirt, sand, snow and ice, loose rock, and tarmac. Watching rallying can be exciting because drivers slide the cars around at high speed, and spend a lot of their time sideways on gravel because this is the fastest way to get round a bend. The times for all the stages are added and the fastest car wins. Because rallying involves driving long distances to get from A to B, rather than around a circuit, the driver needs a co-driver, or navigator, to tell the driver where to go.

Because the drivers are going so fast, there just isn't enough time to 'read' the road; the driver needs to listen to the 'pacenotes' read out by the co-driver. These pacenotes are read out two or three bends ahead, with information such as jumps, water splashes, hill crests and how fast the driver can take the bends. One moment's lapse in concentration from either, and a high speed crash can happen and the rally is lost.

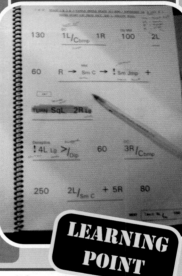

Pacenotes are written in special 'shorthand' code

LEARNING POINT

In rallying, trust is the difference between winning and losing, and between life and death. The driver has to have supreme faith in what the co-driver says about what is to come.

The Christian life is a bit like a rally. There is a finish line (dying and going to Heaven), there are deadly obstacles (Satan tempting us to abandon our faith), many wrong turns which could be taken (anything which takes us away from Jesus), and there is a need to listen carefully to the co-driver (God speaking through the Bible), ignoring distractions (putting Jesus first). Reaching the end of the course will only happen if there is a desire to listen to the Word of God. The Bible is like the pacenotes, as it tells us what is ahead even though we cannot see around the next bend. Christians need to trust God, that what He has said in His Word is true. Not one prophecy (prediction about the future) in the Bible has ever been proved untrue. Christians know they can trust God and His Word.

THE BIBLE SAYS...

'For I know [Jesus] whom I have believed, and am persuaded that he is able to keep *my soul* which I have committed unto him against [or, until] that day [of death, or the end of time].' (2 Timothy 1:12)

'We walk by faith, not by sight.' (2 Corinthians 5:7)

(top) World Rally Championship Hyundai i20 slides sideways at speed on loose gravel

(below left) Driver and co-driver without helmets on, as they drive between the timed sections of the rally. Both need to wear headsets because the car is so noisy they cannot hear each other without them.

(below right) Fiesta rally car kicking up dirt

SPOTLIGHT: *WAY-SPORT*

Rallying to share the Gospel

A quote from John 3:7 is on the car

What is Way-Sport?

Since 1989 Way-Sport (formerly the Alpha and Omega) Christian Motor-sport Team has been taking the Gospel to the motorsport world. The team are based in Suffolk in the UK.

On display at an exhibition

They not only share the Gospel at race meets but also witness by visiting schools and at youth, men's and other events.

Who started the team and why?

Paul Harvey drove tractors for a job, but after he had become a Christian, he had a new confidence that changed his life's course with a thirst for adventure and sharing his faith. He was seeking God's guidance as to what to do with his life. He was good at driving and he felt led to go on a rally driving course, and there he finished top of the class. Then he saw an old rally car for sale at the side of the road and bought it. His brother Mark was a gifted mechanic, and together they started a rally team, with a hand-painted Bible text on the side of their Escort (photos right). Paul's passion isn't rallying, but sharing his faith in Jesus; rallying is his unique way of doing it. The team see this as a ministry, and the car has opened up many opportunities to speak with people about faith. The team is now part of the outreach of Diss Baptist Church.

The team's first car, a Ford Escort Mk2

At a 'men's breakfast' event

Their rally car

The team owns a left-hand-drive 1993 Mk5 Ford Escort RS Cosworth, a turbo-charged 300bhp all-wheel-drive car originally built and used by the Ford Motorsport Team. The Escort RS won several major rallies in the 1990's.

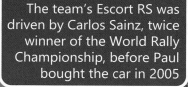

The team's Escort RS was driven by Carlos Sainz, twice winner of the World Rally Championship, before Paul bought the car in 2005

K768 JHK

Team name and Bible quotes

The name of the team—"Way-Sport"—has been chosen because Jesus is the Way—the **only** way to Heaven (see p25).

The Bible text on both sides of the rally car is from John 3:7, which tells those watching that only those who are 'born again' will go to Heaven. To be born again means receiving a new life from God.

When on display the car has the front number plate 'JOHN 316' (photo below), a reference to one of the most well known Bible verses of all (John 3:16). This verse explains that God sent His only Son, Jesus, into the World to give life to those who believe on Him.

Paul Harvey

Way-sport

"Our vision: to take God's message to people in situations that other ministries don't"

DID YOU KNOW?

In the late 1970s, Brazilian F1 driver Alex Ribeiro raced with 'Jesus saves' (or 'Christo Salva') written on his car

JOHN 316

RACE CAR SAFETY
Sensible equipment to prevent harm

WARNING MOTOR SPORT CAN BE DANGEROUS
'DESPITE THE ORGANISERS TAKING ALL REASONABLE PRECAUTIONS, UNAVOIDABLE ACCIDENTS CAN HAPPEN. IN RESPECT OF THESE, YOU ARE PRESENT AT YOUR OWN RISK.'

Modern safety equipment

Hard crash helmet

Harness (multi-point seat belt)

Plumbed-in fire extinguisher (can be started outside the car)

Perspex plastic windows

Engine cut-out switch

Crash-resistant fuel tank

Flameproof overalls, balaclava, gloves

Strap-cutter

Roll cage

Bucket seat

Life is precious

In the early days, no thought was given to safety when cars were built. When men started racing in them, you can imagine the risk of death both to drivers and those watching. It was pretty common for drivers to be thrown out during a crash, as there were no seatbelts. Some were burnt in horrible fires, and some were crushed in their seat as the car turned over.

Over the years, the number of serious crashes has reduced, because measures have been brought in to make race tracks and cars safer. These include all the items shown in the list to the left. Safety equipment thankfully makes death rare, but motorsport is still dangerous.

DID YOU KNOW?
The deadliest crash killed 84 at Le Mans in 1955 when a car catapulted into the crowd

LEARNING POINT

The Bible says that death is the last enemy (1 Corinthians 15:26). Naturally we want to stay alive, and avoid injury and death. But we often have to face trouble in our lives, and we have to face death. The Bible likens this great trouble to being burned in a fire. It says that believers, even if they walk through fire, will not be burned, and the flame won't set light to them (Isaiah 43:2), because they are precious to the Lord. That doesn't of course mean a literal fire, but it does tell us that it is God who protects His people from all harm. His protection is better than any flameproof racing suit.

Although the Lord doesn't always stop His people being actually burned, sometimes he does! Nothing is too hard for Him. Read the story of Shadrach, Meshach and Abed-nego in Daniel 3.

A 1950's Mercedes Grand Prix racing car with no real safety equipment

THE BIBLE SAYS . . .
'And the princes ... saw these men, upon whose bodies the fire had no power.' (Daniel 3:27)

(above) Bucket seats, harnesses, roll cage and harness strap-cutter can be seen in this rally car

(below) AMG Mercedes and Ferrari F1 cars side-by-side. Both cars have a special frame around the cockpit, called a 'halo,' to protect the driver's head from flying objects, like wheels, during a crash.

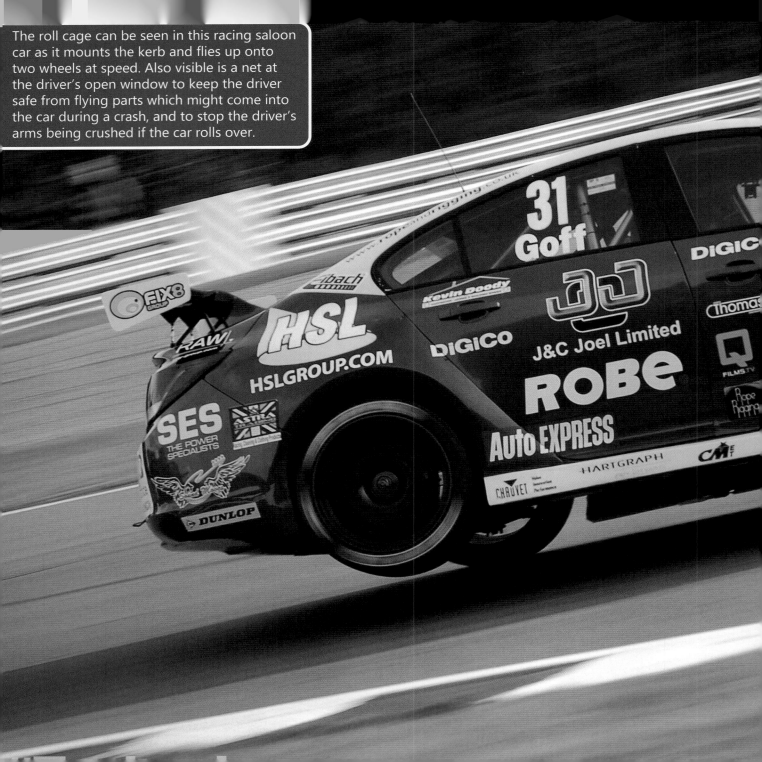

The roll cage can be seen in this racing saloon car as it mounts the kerb and flies up onto two wheels at speed. Also visible is a net at the driver's open window to keep the driver safe from flying parts which might come into the car during a crash, and to stop the driver's arms being crushed if the car rolls over.

This Mini was racing at Brands Hatch in Kent, UK, when it went onto the grass, spun round, flipped, and rolled at least four times into the barrier. The fact that the driver is seen here climbing out is a tribute to safety standards in motorsport.

RACE CAR DESIGN
Preparing for victory isn't just about power

What is needed to make a winning car?

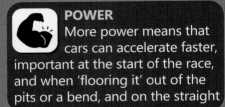 **POWER**
More power means that cars can accelerate faster, important at the start of the race, and when 'flooring it' out of the pits or a bend, and on the straight

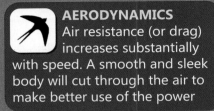 **AERODYNAMICS**
Air resistance (or drag) increases substantially with speed. A smooth and sleek body will cut through the air to make better use of the power

CONTROL
Drivers must be able to 'feel' the limit of what the car can do to get the best from it, and know that it will go exactly where it is pointed

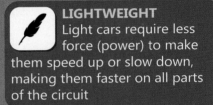 **LIGHTWEIGHT**
Light cars require less force (power) to make them speed up or slow down, making them faster on all parts of the circuit

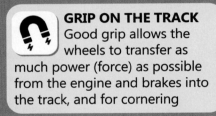 **GRIP ON THE TRACK**
Good grip allows the wheels to transfer as much power (force) as possible from the engine and brakes into the track, and for cornering

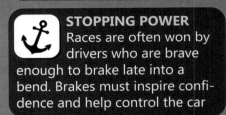 **STOPPING POWER**
Races are often won by drivers who are brave enough to brake late into a bend. Brakes must inspire confidence and help control the car

LEARNING POINT

Race car builders want their car's engine to have as much power as possible. However, there is no point having lots of power, if the car cannot be controlled. The objective—victory—depends on the driver putting the power to good use.

In life, having power brings responsibility. A prime minister, president, or king should not use their power for their own ends, but they must control themselves, using their power wisely.

Jesus is the One who has unlimited power (Matthew 28:18), even over death (Romans 6:9). But see how amazing Jesus is because He controls His power, putting it to the best use. When He was on the Earth, there were wicked people who hated Him, and eventually had him put to death on the cross. How easily Jesus could have killed them with just a word, but He didn't (John 18:6,10-11). Jesus was also taunted to come down off the cross and save Himself, if He was God (Luke 23:35,39). He could have; He had the power. But He didn't. He had a better plan—to use His power to win the victory over Satan when He rose from the dead. O for a heart to praise God that, in love, He uses His power to save sinners!

THE BIBLE SAYS ...
'He began to teach them, that the Son of man [Jesus] must suffer many things ... and be killed, and after three days rise again.' (Mark 8:31)

'Worthy is the Lamb [Jesus] that was slain [killed] to receive power ... and glory.' (Revelation 5:12)

REAR SLICK TYRES
Sticky rubber to stop the wheels spinning when accelerating hard and to resist sliding in the corners

REAR WING
The air rushing over the wing pushes the rear wheels down for better grip at high speed

INTAKE (UPPER)
Cold air to mix with fuel to feed into the engine (colder air gives more power)

BODYWORK AND STRUCTURE
A lightweight and strong rigid carbon fibre shell; includes specially shaped parts to direct the airflow and built to withstand high-speed crashes

Red Bull RB10 Formula One car (2014)

SUSPENSION (INSIDE THE BODY)
Springs to allow movement up and down and dampers to soak up the energy, stopping the wheels bouncing

FRONT SLICK TYRES
Sticky rubber to resist the wheels locking up under braking, or sliding in the corners

ENGINE+GEARBOX
Made of lightweight metal alloys, driving rear wheels, placed at rear for best balance

AIR INTAKES (SIDES)
Cold air is fed through radiators, preventing the engine over-heating

BRAKES (BEHIND EACH WHEEL)
Powerful carbon brakes, which don't 'fade' when hot (they can reach 1,000°C); balance between front and rear brakes is managed by computer

STEERING
Special steering to turn the wheels left and right with only small driver movements, allowing quick turns

FRONT WING
The air rushing over the wing pushes the front wheels down for better grip at high speed

DID YOU KNOW?
Lots of race series set rules for car design to keep the racing close and exciting. In F1 for 2022, cars must weigh at least 795kg. Engineers still make the car as light as possible, though, and then add ballast (dead weight) near the ground, to make the cars as stable as possible

AMG Mercedes Formula 1 car. The complex shape of the front wing can be clearly seen here (main photo)—it has been designed using a computer to get smooth air flow

RACE TEAMS
Full-time professional motorsport

(right) A pit stop, which can take place in under 5 seconds, requires a small army, with everyone working closely together

(below right) Boring, but essential—every tyre and wheel needs carefully checking

(below far right) Teamwork and commitment can lead to victory; here is Fernando Alonso winning the British GP in 2011

No room for a half-hearted approach

Formula 1 (F1) racing is considered to be the ultimate in motorsport. All through the winter, when no racing takes place, work carries on quickly to design, build, develop and test a new car for the next season. No expense is spared in developing the most advanced designs, using computer-aided design, where the engineers test many different ideas. Then the builders make the parts out of carbon fibre or metal alloys, and the cars are assembled. The cars are driven hard round a track, by special test drivers, and the performance is monitored by computers and analysed by technicians. Meanwhile, the pit crew who service the cars and change the wheels practice over and over again. All of this requires a large team to be employed full-time, working through the week; they cannot just turn up on the day of the race, and hope for the best. The whole team is committed, and set up to focus on winning races. A slack attitude just will not do!

F1 drivers, like Sebastian Vettel (on the right) work closely with the team to get the best out of the car

LEARNING POINT

Do you go to church or chapel on Sundays? It is a good thing if you do, as the Bible says that it is hearing the Gospel which leads to salvation. But going to church services doesn't, by itself, save anyone, in the same way that sleeping in a garage doesn't make you a car. When God truly saves someone, there should be evidence that He has worked in their lives. They should not be 'holy' on Sundays, and then live carelessly, or foolishly, the rest of the week (Matthew 7:16-20). If they realise they are sinners, and that there is a day coming when Jesus will return, they should live as though He is the most important thing; they should be committed; they should be diligent to seek God daily. The Lord does not want part-time Christians. Unlike the race team, where winning is not certain, victory <u>is</u> certain for those on the Lord's side! (1 Corinthians 15:57)

THE BIBLE SAYS ...
'If any man will come after me [Jesus], let him deny himself, and take up his cross daily, and follow me.' (Luke 9:23)

DID YOU KNOW?
The fastest 'pit stop' to change all four wheels took just 1.82 seconds, by Red Bull Racing in Brazil in 2019

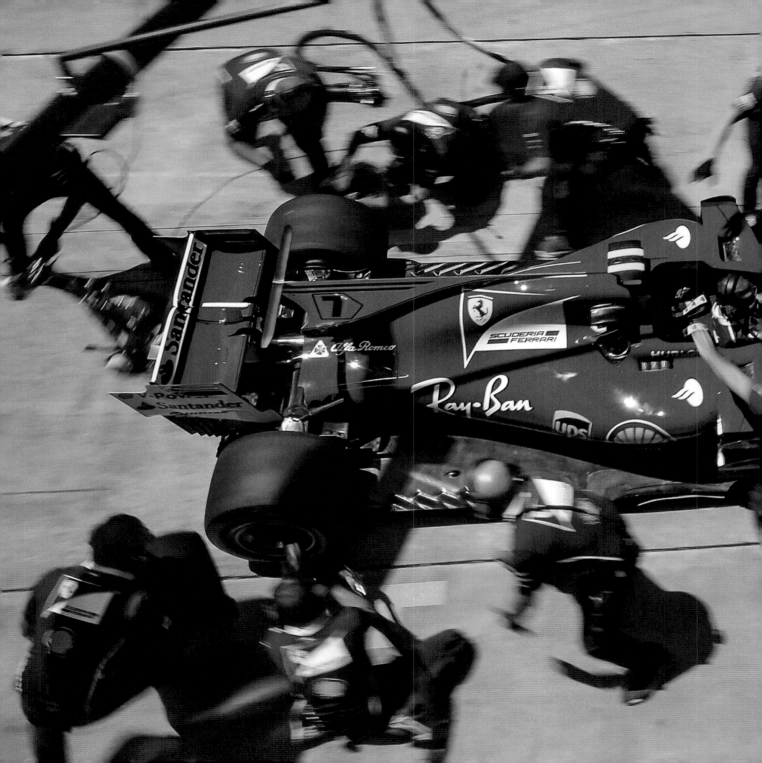

A Scuderia Ferrari team practices a pit stop to change wheels. There are three people for each wheel—one removing/replacing the wheel nut, one to remove the old wheel and another to put the new wheel on; plus one front and one rear to lift the car on jacks.

LE MANS 24HRS
The famous French endurance race

1966: A Ford GT40 on its way to a famous victory, when Ford beat Ferrari for the first time

What does it take to win Le Mans?

Most car races last a few minutes, or possibly a few hours. Le Mans requires cars to travel as far as they can in 24 hours, which of course means driving through the day and the night, in any weather conditions.

Historically each car had only 2 drivers, though now it is 3, and they take it in turns. The hard part is trying to sleep during your break, which might be only 2-4 hours, and then waking up to get behind the wheel to drive in darkness at over 200mph. Although there are other 24 hour races, such as Daytona in the USA, what makes Le Mans especially difficult is that the race circuit is in parts a collection of normal roads, and not a dedicated race circuit, and as a result is much more dangerous. A moment's lapse in concentration could end in disaster, and there have been serious crashes (see p56).

The other challenge which drivers face is that racing is hard on the cars as well as the drivers. If the driver pushes too hard, their car could break. But if they go too slow, they may not win.

Experience is needed to decide on the best strategy for winning, and this requires calm thinking, no matter how tired they are.

LEARNING POINT

Sometimes we can be really enthusiastic when we start something new, like a new school, or a new job. But we might be reminded that life is a marathon, not a sprint! It is good to be enthusiastic, but we if we are serious about success, we need to keep at it day after day. We need to be steady and focus on the end goal. This is the approach needed to win Le Mans.

It is the same in a Christian's life. Jesus told a parable about people who started off their religious life well, but before long they had lost their initial enthusiasm, and had got distracted or had difficulty (the Parable of the Sower, Mark 4:1-20). John Bunyan's Pilgrim's Progress also showed how important it is for Christians to keep looking to God day after day, to endure unto the end, for the prize of being with Jesus in Heaven. Praise God, that Jesus gives His people the strength they need to endure (John 6:37-40).

DID YOU KNOW?
Le Mans is the oldest endurance race in the World. The first one was held in 1923.

THE BIBLE SAYS...
'He that shall endure unto the end, the same shall be saved.' (Matthew 24:13)

(above) Racing at night is especially difficult and requires bright headlights to see far enough down the famous Mulsanne Straight where cars can top 200mph. The carbon brake discs are glowing as this car brakes hard before a bend.

(left) An Aston Martin stops in the pits for a driver change and refuel

(below) The need to drive for so long in any conditions favours cars with an enclosed cabin

NASCAR
American high-octane oval racing

DID YOU KNOW?
NASCAR stands for the National Association of Stock Car Automobile Racing. With speeds of up to 200mph, it is dangerous, but no drivers have been killed since 7-time championship winner Dale Earnhardt died in 2001.

No right turns

In the UK and Europe, most race tracks have a unique shape with lots of bends—both left and right hand turns. This puts the emphasis on handling in the bends. In the USA, oval circuit racing is the dominant motorsport, and there are several famous tracks including the Indianapolis Motor Speedway and Daytona International Speedway. These tracks run anti-clockwise and only feature gradual left turns, normally on banking to carry more speed around the track.

One of the race series is more popular than F1 in the US—NASCAR. The NASCAR company runs 1,500+ races at 100+ tracks in 48 US states, Mexico and Canada. When started in 1948, the idea was that cars would be raced 'stock' (as they came out of the factory), but after a few years, modifications were allowed for safety and performance. By the mid-1960s the vehicles were purpose-built race cars, but with a body shape resembling 'stock' cars. The racing is very close, as drivers can readily overtake on the wide track.

A typical NASCAR race car

LEARNING POINT

Because the cars generally only need to turn left on large oval tracks, they are set up to follow the track round—to keep going in the direction required.

When Adam and Eve were created by God, they had a happy relationship with Him. He had made them to have their desires always towards Him—looking to God, and following Him. They were built that way, like NASCAR cars, whose builders have set them up to keep 'on track.' But when Adam and Eve sinned, they did not want to follow the course God had set; they turned out of the way, to please themselves, as do you and I by nature. We are like a NASCAR that has crashed and been twisted out of shape. Adam and Eve's sin means we all sin; all of us are twisted. We need fixing. Who can fix us? There is only One: Jesus. He can give us the desire to follow Him.

THE BIBLE SAYS . . .
'By one man's disobedience [Adam's] many were made sinners, so by the obedience of one [Christ] shall many be made righteous.' (Romans 5:19)

(above) The green flag moment at the start of the race, here at Dover Downs Raceway in 2007

(below) A high-speed smash on the banking. The outside (upper) walls of the tracks are now fitted with crash barriers, as can be seen here, to make it safer.

SUPERCARS

The most desirable cars—for those with big budgets

Porsche 911 are at the very cheap end of supercars, but if you want the latest model GT3 RS you will still need £140,000

The 1,000bhp Bugatti Veyron

How deep are your pockets?

For some, owning a supercar is a *status symbol*—something that shows off to everyone else how much money you have. Ferraris, in their bright red paintwork and with the prancing horse badge on the bonnet, have for decades been a schoolboy's dream machine.

However, there is now a great deal of choice if you have deep pockets, with cars from Bugatti, Lamborghini, Aston Martin and McLaren all costing over $2 million.

The most expensive street-legal production car is the Koenigsegg CCXR Trevita, costing nearly $5 million. The high price is because the paint contains diamond dust!

Koenigsegg CCXR

You certainly have to be rich to own a new supercar. Some people mistakenly think that, if you are a Christian, it is bad to be rich. The Bible nowhere teaches this, but it does teach about the risks of being wealthy. We too easily focus on the riches, and not on the One who has given them! It has been said, "There is no problem owning stuff, the problem is when the stuff owns you!" Sadly many rich people are obsessed with what they possess, yet never give any thought to their souls and what will happen when they die. They are never content. The Apostle Paul said to Timothy (in 1 Timothy 6:17-19) that he was to instruct those Christians in the Church who were rich, to not be proud or rely on their money, but to rely on God, who has given us all these things to enjoy freely. They should do good with their money, being ready to give generously and be ready to help others.

If you had enough money to buy a Ferrari, would you? It is a blessing if you can say, 'No.' God can make us content with what we own, and give us a heart to do good with our money.

THE BIBLE SAYS...

'What shall it profit a man, if he shall gain the whole world, and lose his own soul? Or what shall a man give in exchange for his soul?' (Mark 8:36-37)

'Godliness with contentment is great gain.' (1 Timothy 6:6)

DID YOU KNOW?

The Bugatti Veyron 16.4 Super Sport is the fastest production car (268mph top speed)

This Ferrari LaFerrari has 'butterfly doors' and with its petrol/electric hybrid engine takes just 6.9 secs to reach 200kph (124mph)

GLOSSARY

Driving home the meaning of technical words in this book

4x4: Four-by-four; the vehicle has 4 wheels, and all 4 of them are 'driving wheels', that is, the engine powers all 4 wheels. The term 4x4 is normally used for vehicles designed for mostly off-road use. When all the wheels are driven by the engine, the vehicle is more likely to get grip.

Accelerator: The pedal used to 'rev' the engine (see below for 'rev'). Max accelerator='full throttle.'

All-wheel-drive: Same as '4x4,' but the term often applies to vehicles designed mostly for road use.

bhp: Brake horse power, a standard measure of an engine's power output. The metric version of bhp is PS (PS=Pferdestärke, the German for horsepower). 100bhp=101PS. Typical family car has 75 to 150bhp.

Cabbie: Taxi driver; taxis are actually called taxicabs (tax=to charge; cab=cabriolet, an old carriage).

Cabin: The passenger compartment, the part of the car where the people sit, enclosed by a roof.

Carbon fibre: A lightweight, stiff material made by glueing together many layers of thin sheets of fibres.

Clutch: Spinning plates which separate from each other to allow the engine crankshaft (power output) to temporarily split from the gearbox, allowing the driver to change gear, or stop the vehicle without stalling.

Congestion: (Informally: traffic jam) A build-up of traffic because the volume (of cars) is too great for the road capacity (the amount of cars that the road can manage).

F1: Formula One, highest-profile international race series. Sometimes called GP / Grand Prix (Prize) racing.

Gearbox: Gears (cogs) which take the spinning output from the engine and slow it down ready to use at the wheels. There are a number of gears to allow the driver to select for the right speed.

High octane (fuel): Fuel which produces more power. Used as an expression meaning powerful, energetic.

Hybrid engine: Usually a petrol engine working together with electric batteries to drive the vehicle.

Left-hand-drive: The driver sits on the left hand side of the car, for use in countries where cars drive on the right hand side of the road, including North America and within (the continent of) Europe.

Manual (car): (US: 'stick') A car where the driver has to select the right gear, using the gearstick. There are normally 4 to 6 forward gears and one for reverse (backwards). 'Automatic' cars are ones where the driver does not have to change gear—the car is designed to do this without the driver's input.

Pits: The area of a race circuit dedicated to servicing race vehicles, for use before, during or after the race.

Racing circuit: (or race track) Normally a dedicated track for racing, which forms a continuous loop enabling races to run over several laps (1 lap = once round). Temporary circuits can be built on normal roads.

Rev / revs: One revolution is when the engine crankshaft (the rotating spine of the engine which transmits the power) rotates once. To 'rev' the engine is to make it do more 'revs per minute' (rpm).

Roll cage: Shaped metal tubes welded inside a car to prevent the roof being crushed if it rolls over.

Roundabout: As the name suggests, a junction where traffic goes around a central island.

Traffic lights: (or traffic signals) Red, amber and green lights placed at a junction, which drivers must obey. The purpose is to have each road take it in turns, to help capacity, and/or for road safety.

Satnav: Satellite navigation. Special satellites in the sky send out a signal which is picked up by the satnav device (which might be a mobile phone). Any three satellites allow the device to calculate its position.

Single track: A road which is not wide enough for two vehicles to pass each other, except in a passing place.

Slick tyres: Racing tyres with no tread (grooves), to maximise grip. Not suitable for use in wet weather.

Speedometer: (or speedo) A dial/gauge or digital readout of the vehicle's speed displayed for the driver.

Stall: When a petrol or diesel engine stops unintentionally, and needs to be restarted.

Turbocharged: Engines where the fuel/air mixture is pushed into it rather than sucked into it. The exhaust gas drives a turbocharger, spinning at high speed, to pump the fuel/air in, increasing power.

V8: An engine with 8 cylinders (see diagram below for a cylinder) arranged in a V shape when viewed from the front of the engine. Typical car engines have 4 cyclinders, but some have 3, 5, 6 or even 12.

How a typical car motor works - the 'four stroke' engine

STROKE: **1st** (down)   **2nd** (up)   **3rd** (down)   **4th** (up)

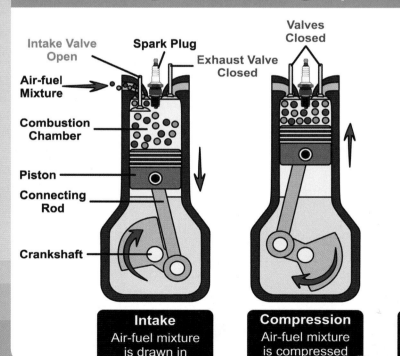

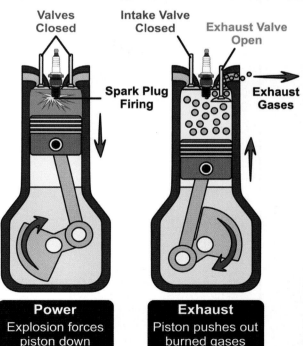

Intake	Compression	Power	Exhaust
Air-fuel mixture is drawn in	Air-fuel mixture is compressed	Explosion forces piston down	Piston pushes out burned gases

Published by: Day One Publications, Ryelands Rd, Leominster, HR6 8NZ
sales@dayone.co.uk
www.dayone.co.uk

Answers to questions on page 12:

1. No entry (Exodus 40:35)
2. One-way street (Deuteronomy 28:7)
3. Steep hill downwards ahead (Luke 8:33)
4. No U-turn (Deuteronomy 17:16)
5. No overtaking (Amos 9:10)
6. Risk of falling or fallen rocks ahead (Revelation 6:16)
7. Weight limit (Luke 11:46)
8. Roundabout ahead (Joshua 6:3)
9. No left turn (Deuteronomy 5:32)
10. Width restriction (Matthew 7:14)

Answers to questions on page 30:

1. B (2 Samuel 23:5—spoken by David)
2. C (Jeremiah 31:33—to God's people)
3. A (Genesis 9:16—to Noah and all living creatures)

Copyright © Mark Philpott 2022
ISBN 978-1-84625-715-5

Bible quotes are from the Authorised (King James) Version. If words have been replaced for clarity, these are shown in *italics*. If words have been inserted, these are shown in square brackets [ ].

Reference to organisations or persons does not imply endorsement by the Author or Publisher of their views or activities. Likewise, inclusion of an organisation or individual does not imply their endorsement of this book or its contents.

ACKNOWLEDGEMENTS

Recognising help given and the sources of the photos in this book

Key: p=page number pp=pages T=top B=bottom L=left R=right C=centre

Mombasa Mission https://mombasamission.com
Thanks to James Gudgeon for assisting with 'Mission Support,' and permission to use the photographs on **pp46-47**.

Open Doors https://www.opendoorsuk.org https://www.opendoorsusa.org
Thanks for permission to include excerpts from their website for the section 'The Bible Smuggler,' for assistance with the text, and supply of the three images at the top of **p45** (logo, image of Brother Andrew, and of 'God's Smuggler').

Way-Sport Christian Motorsport Team Facebook @waysportcmt
Thanks to Steve Dennis and Paul Harvey for the team photographs on **pp54-55**; all are © Way-Sport CMT.

UK Department for Transport https://www.gov.uk/guidance/traffic-sign-images#terms-and-conditions
UK road signs are reproduced under the Open Government License. All of the images are © Crown Copyright.

Licensed by Creative Commons www.creativecommons.org/licenses + www.flickr.com
License details available at above web address. Unless noted in square brackets after each attribution, image license will be 'CC BY 2.0'; abbreviations are used where the license type differs: SA='CC BY-SA 2.0'; ND='CC BY-ND 2.0'; 3='CC BY-3.0', etc. All photos have been sourced from **flickr.com**, except those suffixed '[W]' which are sourced from **https://commons.wikimedia.org/**.

Front cover: T "Neste Oil Rally 2010 - Jari-Matti Latvala in shakedown" by kallerna [SA3, W]; B "FERRARI SF90 / Sebastian Vettel / GER / Scuderia Ferrari" by Artes Max [SA]; **p1** "KYN_0749 WRC Rally d'Italia Sardegna (2011)" by Kyn Wai Chung [ND]; **pp2-3** "Knickerbrook 2" by Lee Fraser; **pp4-5** (map background) "Ban đo giao thông đuong bo khu vuc KONTUM - PLEIKU - AN KHÊ (BÌNH ĐỊNH) ngày nay" by manhhai; **p6** "Mini Cooper S, Goodwood Festival of Speed 2017" by Neil; **p8** "Speed Camera" by Geoff Henson; **p9** "Wrapped up warm" by Allen Watkin [SA]; **p11** TR "Information overload!" by John K Thorne; B "Audi TT RS Coupe" by The NRMA; **p13** TL "Highway 28 sign between Farson Wyoming and Seedskadee NWR" by USFWS Mountain-Prairie; CL "Road Sign - South Africa" by Christopher Griner [ND]; C "Warning sign ..." (multiple animals) by Bernard DUPONT [SA]; C "Please brake for snakes" by Mike Bowler; CR "Pengions Crossing" by Geerd-Olaf Freyer [SA]; TR "Kangaroo sign" by Nicolò Bonazzi [ND]; **p14** T "Felix Cats Eyes" by Paul Wordingham; **p15** T "Monte-Carlo WRC 2014 ES2" by Aurélien JEANNE [SA]; **p16** "MY TRAVELS" by whologwhy; **p17** "Big Ben (DSC00025)" by Allan Patrick [SA]; TL "London - Cabs - Rushhoure" by Micha Kaiser [ND]; **p18** T "CIU officers examine BK35" by Highways Patrol Images; B "ambulance (3)" by bertknot [SA]; **p19** T "Abu Dhabi Police - Lykan Hypersport (Official Press)" by Felix Berndt Photography; B "M5 Car Fire" by Tony Hisgett; **p22** L "Bathurst 1000 V8 Supercars, Holden GTS" by # [SA]; R "Outside the patrol car" by Oregon Department of Transportation; **p23** "IMG_3199" (Gatso) by Tom Page [SA]; **pp24-25** "Loop 202 and US 60 Interchange (3)" by Alan Stark [SA]; **p24** B "mtwofive105.jpg" (M25) by osde8info [SA]; **p25** R "Quiet Country Lanes" by 35mmMan; **pp26-27** "Golden Gate" by Mike McBey; **p28** "File:Baldwin_Street.JPG" by Samuel Böcker [SA4, W]; **p29** TL "Gambia" by Jurgen; TR "Monument Valley" by Mobilus In Mobili [SA]; B "Trollstigen- Troll's way" by Karen Blaha [SA]; **p31** T "NEW DISCOVERY SVX: LAND ROVER REVEALS ALL-TERRAIN CHAMPION AT FRANKFURT IAA" by Land Rover MENA; B "Porsche cars" by JCT 600; **p32** "1974 Austin Mini 1275GT" by Graham Robertson; **p33** T "You have got to be joking me..." by Charles; B "101/365+1 On Tow" by Dave Crosby [SA]; **p34** "H5550 PO68YHU Alexandra Sophia Eddie Stobart" by EDDIE; **p35** T "Truck Spotting on the A29 @ The Shell Services Numansdorp..." by Rab Lawrence; TR "BL57740 (18.08.09, Motorvej 501, Viby J)DSC_7311_Balancer" by Lav Ulv; CR "BL81468 (18.08.21, Østhavnsvej, Sumatravej)DSC_8354_Balancer" by Lav Ulv; **p36** from TL to BR: "Mack MR" by Jason Lawrence; "AW82857 (18.05.08, Motorvej 501, Viby J)DSC_7378_Balancer" by Lav Ulv; "ROYAL MAIL PN08RUC 240510" by EDDIE [ND]; "Renault Car Transporter Stva Car & Commercial" by lee bristol [SA]; "PX09 XRF, a JET Fuels DAF CF tanker" by Ray Forster [ND]; "CEMEX DAF CF, GN58 KSF" by Ray Forster [ND]; "A MAN TGS livestock transporter, NV60 KHY" by Ray Forster [ND]; "Mobile Crane" by Ozzy Delaney; "Bidvest 3663 SN06 HHZ" by Glen Wallace [SA]; "VN89088 (Falck) (13.09.06-2) (med XN32887 (ambulance))_Balancer" by Lav Ulv; "Winter Fleet at Full Strength" by Scottish Government; "Elite Traveller" by apollo motorhomes [ND]; **p37** from TL to BR: "Fire Engine 2" by Tony Hisgett; "BD87615 (18.07.03, Motorvej 501, Viby J)DSC_3613_Balancer" by Lav Ulv; "BG83160 (19.03.28,

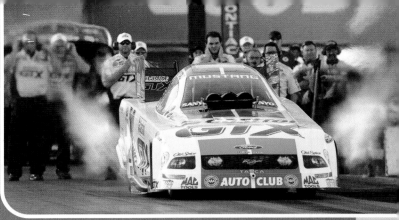

A 'funny car' dragster at full throttle, as flames pour from the huge side exhausts as it starts down the 'quarter mile' strip. The fastest funny car did the quarter in 3.9 seconds and crossed the line at 322mph!

Motorvej 501, Viby J)DSC_6506FlickrR" by Lav Ulv; "XP95363 (13.04.16)_Balancer" (container) by Lav Ulv; "Big Winch for My 1st Shot of Grampians New Rear Steer 4Axel Low Loader" by Rab Lawrence; "54122-MC -1 250714 CPS" (cement) by Chris Sampson [SA]; "Stockbridge" (skip) by Herry Lawford; "ICC Champions Trophy 2017 - Edgbaston - Event Pass Holders Only Ahead" by Elliott Brown [SA]; **p38** "A Pollard Volvo FH" by Barry Lewis; **p39** TL "Just Put It On Top" by Christoph Rupprecht [SA]; TR "Overloaded" by Dan Benedict Banaag; BL "Overloaded" (tuktuk) by Prashant Ram [ND]; BR "444 (26)" by SIM USA [SA]; **pp40-41** (4 photos) "Subsea 7 towheads in Wick" by Glen Wallace [SA]; **p45** "VW Beetle in the rain" by Mark Vletter [SA]; **p47** T "DSC_4816" by Draco2008; B "Child Abuse Prevention Car Show" by Rockin'Rita [ND]; **p49** C "1963 Morris Mini-Cooper Monte Carlo" by David Merrett; TR "Works Mini Cooper S DJB 93B" by Andrew Basterfield [SA]; B "Beaulieu 2013" by Sammieee; **pp50-51** "mini crowd" by Ian Fearing [ND]; **p51** inset "Splashin' around" by jason goulding; **p52** "112/365" by Gordon Flood; **p53** T "File:Rally_Italy_2016_001.jpg" by Hyundai Motorsport [3, W]; BL "rally montecarlo hirvonen" by mauro; BR "File:Ford Fiesta RS WRC (Gabriel Pozzo y Daniel Stillo).jpg" by Alejandro Zurcher [SA4, W]; **p55** TR "1997" by Box Repsol; **p56** T "Danger" by Phil Whitehouse; B "Goodwood Festival of Speed 2014" by Paul Williams; **p57** "Charles Leclerc, Ferrari SF90 holds off Lewis Hamilton, Mercedes F1 W10, 2019 Italian Grand Prix, Monza, 8th September" by Interceptor73; **pp58-59** "Jack Goff BTCC Final Round Qualifying 2013" by Rowan Harrison [SA]; **p59** BR "#747 Kelvin Edgar - Mini 7 S Class Championship - Brands Hatch GP - British GT Race 7" by Mark Seymour; **p61** "Edmonton Motor Show 2014" (background removed, annotations added) by IQRemix [SA]; **pp62-63** "DSC_8235" by Thomas Ormston; **p63** TR "No.44 / Lewis Hamilton / Mercedes AMG Petronas F1 Team" by Keisuke Kariya; **p64** "F1 - Red Bull - Sebastian Vettel" by Jake Archibald; **p65** T "DSC_2369" by tigerlily07; BL "Red Bull Racing - F1 Pit Garage" by Jitesh Jagadish; BR "ALONSO BRITISH GP 2011 (4)" by Bertho RF1 [SA]; **p68** "24 heures du Mans 1966" by ZANTAFIO56 [SA]; **p69** T "24 Hours of Le Mans 2011 - Qualifying 1 - RML HPD #36" by Alessandro Prada [SA]; B "European Le Mans Series" by United Autosports [SA]; **p70** "Mad Max" by Matt Lewis [SA]; **p71** T "The Green Flag" by Jasen Miller; **p72** T "GT3 RS green" by Ben [SA]; C "Bugatti Veyron" by Thank You (22 Millions+) views; B "Europe 2011" by Ben Ramirez; **p73** "Laferrari" by Ben [SA]; **pp76-77** 2018_F1_Qual-206-2-Edit by Joe McGowan; **p79** "Ashley Force" by Ford Racing; **p80** "Lifeguards" by Brian Roberts; **Back cover**: CL "H5514 PO68YGF Damia Natashia Eddie Stobart" by EDDIE [ND]; CR "Ada Cat" by interestedbystandr; T "FERRARI SF90 / Charles Leclerc / MCO / Scuderia Ferrari" by Artes Max [SA].

Icons from the Noun Project https://thenounproject.com

Front cover/p3 Steering Wheel by Zahroe; **p4** Driver by Adriano Emerick; **p8** Spectacles by juli, Moustache by Iconicgr; **p12** Road Sign by Marco Livolsi; **p14** Owl by Oksana Latysheva; **p16** Brain by suhyeon Jung; **p18** Siren by Adrien Coquet; **p30** Keys by Gregor Cresnar; **p32** Sale by MRK; **p34** Truck by David Khai; **p38** Electronic Weight Scale by Vector Portal; **p40** Elephant by Iconographer; **p42** Africa by Yohann Berger; **p44** Guard by Rflor; **p46** Space Invader by Melvin Salas; **p48** Winner by Creative Stall; **p52** Forest by Design Circle; **p56** Helmet by Ayub Irawan; **p60** Feather by sarah; Biceps by Vectors Point; Anchor by Alina Oleynik; Swallow by Anand Prahlad; Magnet by IconPai; Control by DinosoftLab; **p64** Team by OliM; **p68** Day And Night by Dániel Aczél; **p70** Uncle Sam Hat by Melvin Salas; **p72** Sunglasses by Stanislav Levin.

Shutterstock Stock images available from https://www.shutterstock.com

p11 TL Michael Jung; **p15** B Darren Baker; **pp20-21** Firefighter Montreal; **p33** patat; **p57** T FernandoV; **pp66-67** Abdul Razak Latif; **p71** B Grindstone Media Group; **p75** udaix.

Thanks to those who have helped in various ways especially Henry Pearce, and Andy and Harry Taylor. A particular thank you to my long-suffering family, who again have taken on a lot of my household jobs to enable me to prepare this book!

Other books in the series include:

Flight School

Farm School

Battle School

Contact DayOne for more details

More titles being added to the series